DARTM[O]
and Kingswear

Chips Barber—

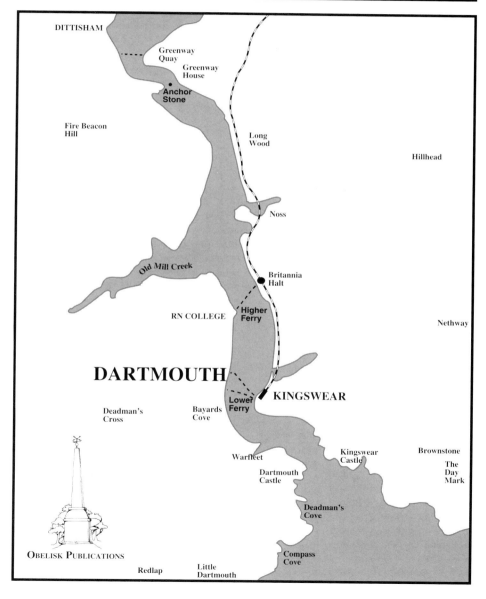

DITTISHAM

Greenway
Quay

Greenway
House

●Anchor
Stone

Fire Beacon
Hill

Long
Wood

Hillhead

Noss

Old Mill Creek

●Britannia
Halt

RN COLLEGE

Higher
Ferry

Nethway

DARTMOUTH

Lower
Ferry

KINGSWEAR

Deadman's
Cross

Bayards
Cove

Warfleet

Kingswear
Castle

Brownstone

The
Day
Mark

Dartmouth
Castle

Deadman's
Cove

OBELISK PUBLICATIONS

Redlap

Little
Dartmouth

Compass
Cove

ALSO BY THE AUTHOR
From The Dart to The Start
Around & About Salcombe
The South Hams
The Great Little Dartmoor Book / The Great Little Exeter Book
The Great Little Plymouth Book / The Great Little Totnes Book
The Lost City of Exeter
Diary of a Dartmoor Walker / Diary of a Devonshire Walker
Beautiful Dartmoor / Beautiful Exeter
Torbay in Colour / Plymouth in Colour
Made in Devon *(with David FitzGerald)*
Dark and Dastardly Dartmoor *(with Sally Barber)*
Weird and Wonderful Dartmoor *(with Sally Barber)*
Ghastly and Ghostly Devon *(with Sally Barber)*
The Ghosts of Exeter *(with Sally Barber)*
Ten Family Walks on Dartmoor *(with Sally Barber)*
Ten Family Walks in East Devon *(with Sally Barber)*
Burgh Island and Bigbury Bay *(with Judy Chard)*
Tales of the Teign *(with Judy Chard)*
Dawlish and Dawlish Warren
Torquay / Paignton / Brixham
Around & About Seaton and Beer
Around & About Sidmouth
Around & About Teignmouth and Shaldon
Topsham Past and Present

OTHER TITLES ABOUT THIS AREA
Under Sail Through S Devon and Dartmoor, *Raymond B. Cattell*
Walks in the South Hams, *Brian Carter*

For further details of these or any of our titles, please send an SAE to Obelisk Publications at the address below, or telephone Exeter 468556.

**All photos by or belonging to Chips Barber
Map by Sally Barber**

*First published in 1994
by Obelisk Publications, 2 Church Hill, Pinhoe, Exeter, Devon
Designed by Chips and Sally Barber
Typeset by Sally Barber
Printed in Great Britain by
Maslands Ltd, Tiverton, Devon*

**All Rights Reserved
© Chips Barber**

DARTMOUTH
and Kingswear

Every year thousands of people visit Dartmouth and most of them like the relaxed mood of the place so much that they come back time and time again. This little book is meant for them and also for those who live here who would like to know more about the area without having too detailed a history lesson.

The picturesque nature of the setting of both Dartmouth and Kingswear has often caught the eye of the rich and of the famous. A "Who's Who" of visitors to this area would include some famous names, many of whom will get a passing mention in this book.

We will also discover why Dartmouth is the prettiest place in the world, how some of Agatha Christie's mysteries were solved here, what 'shock' you got from dialling 'Dartmouth 3', and how they might, just conceivably, bring on a real 'sub' at a football match!

The idea of the book wasn't to write another history of the town because others, before me, have been along that chronological road and their determined, dedicated and detailed researches remain for you to consult when you want to learn even more about this special haven at the mouth of the Dart. Here, then, is a light-hearted look at just some of the many ingredients that go to make up this pair of settlements. Hopefully the pictures and the prose will reflect the mood and atmosphere of this wonderful part of Devon. Let's start with a walkabout of about a mile around the older part of Dartmouth town.

As I cannot personally accompany you around, the next best thing is to get you to do this town trail and fill your mind with a mixture of trivia and watered down history.

Dartmouth is a wonderful place so we are sure that you will enjoy your romp but don't get too sidetracked by the numerous inns and eating places along the way. That's always best left to the very end when you most need some reviving!

The best place to start is where the North Embankment meets the South Embankment. The obvious landmark to start at is the station with no railway lines, now the Station Restaurant. The trivia-type question of "which town has a station but no railway?" is answered here. In the past tickets were purchased for rail journeys that began on the other side at Kingswear. You may just see a train billowing great clouds of steam, sending grown men into a state of euphoria, across the water. This is the Paignton and Dartmouth Railway (or something along those lines). An examination of the menu shows that the restaurant is aware of its railway heritage for it includes 'Great Western' burgers on the menu.

Across the road on the railings, by the Boatfloat, is a sign that commemorates the 125th anniversary (1864–1989) of the arrival of the railway service in Dartmouth, in particular to commemorate the landing place of the first passengers to use the railway.

On the opposite corner is a fine building called York House, built in 1893, now Forbuoys, a newsagent's shop. It stands on the corner of the Quay and South Embankment and is probably one of the most photographed newsagent's shops in Britain!

We are going to head south, down river, as people associate this as leading to warmer and more exotic climes. The buildings that run along this stretch are ones that have caused people and travel writers to say that Dartmouth has the appearance of a Rhenish town. They make an impressive waterfront. Although we will not mention every building, the famous 'Carved Angel' restaurant is next door, complete with some colourful faces, with a variety of expressions, to adorn the building.

Just beyond is Raleigh Court, which was once the Raleigh Hotel. It was the first bulding constructed on the new embankment in 1889. It is a colourful edifice with its four blue dragons each with a fiery red tongue. Every year thousands promenade along this walkway without ever thinking to gaze up at the wonders above. Perhaps they are mindful of the presence of overhead seagulls who are always wont to bestow good luck, or something else, on hapless visitors. Who knows?

The next group of dragons adorn the River Dart Cafe (Embankment House), just a little way farther along the embankment, and are kept company by what appears to be some lions.

Beyond Hauley Road, named after a famous Dartmouth man and contemporary of Chaucer, is the Cottage

Hospital. This was opened in 1894, and financed by public subscription. Its new wing was added in 1974 and financed by monies raised by the League of Friends. Continue along the South Embankment.

There is a danger when following town trails like this that you only notice what has been pointed out and it would be a sacrilege not to enjoy the river views with Dartmouth Castle, now evident, jutting out into the mouth of the river – but don't trip over the memorial stone about 40 yards beyond the Harbour Office, once the post office! It commemorates the opening of the embankment by HRH Duchess of Kent on 24 September 1986. Also you may need to watch out for the fishing lines of those who dabble in piscatorial pursuits as you approach the attractive cottage at Tippers Quay at the end of this straight stretch. The cannon here was brought back as a trophy of war from the Crimea. It rests a long way from the foundry in Russia where it was originally cast in 1826.

Well you only have a singular cannon to the left of you so head to the right. At the end of the road, where an ice cream emporium tempts town trailers to temporarily stop their tour, turn left. Do not get aboard the Lower Ferry but head past the ancient Agincourt House, now an antique shop, and the Dartmouth Arms.

Now we reach another place with its own dragon but you must look for it and not feel too 'brassed off' if you don't find it! Bayards Cove is missed by many visitors who settle for a walk around the town and that part of the waterfront where the river ferries operate. This is an attractive and

pleasing-to-the-eye line of buildings, a place to sit and watch all the comings and goings in the estuary. It has also been popular with film makers but treat this as a 'trailer' for all will be revealed later.

In the past it was the practice of coal-lumpers to spend time here. In Harper's guide book to South Devon written in 1907 he says: *"At Bayard's Cove in especial, the coal-lumpers, the boatmen, and the generally idle sit on the quay walls in the sun, or lean against them, keeping them up. The coal-lumpers work perhaps sixteen or twenty hours at a stretch, coaling the steamers that come into the port, and then want no more work for a month. They laze away the days, run up a score at the nearest pub, and groan if by chance they see another job coming around the corner..."*

For the more modern idler there are a series of benches here on which to sit. They are all put there in loving memory of some dearly departed relative or friend who would have had fond memories of sitting in such an historic location. Apart from the many period films and television programmes made here there have also been some key real life episodes, some shaping the wider history of the world. A stone unveiled here in 1957 gives us details of the *Mayflower* and *Speedwell*'s departure, in August 1620, and subsequent return when problems arose after about three hundred miles on the journey out. The vessels both put back to Plymouth before only the larger *Mayflower* (180 tons) completed the historic transatlantic journey.

The Custom House has a long history, the date 1739 above its door just a statistic that fronts centuries of conversations of maritime trade, above board and otherwise.

The observant will find two plaques of former insurance companies, the West of England being one of them. There is also a splendid example of a Negretti Zambra Barometer that was given to the mariners of Dartmouth by John Hardy, Esq., and MP of Dunstall Hall in Staffordshire in November 1860. A fast falling barometer was not a time to put to sea, whereas one that registered a high reading was often matched by calm conditions. The barometer has been restored, repaired and maintained by the Friends of Bayards Cove. It has been suggested that Bayard might derive from a Germanic word that means 'heavy horse'. Therefore this could well have been the dock where heavy horses, bound for war service in foreign parts, were loaded onto ships.

At the end of Bayards Cove enter the diminutive Bayards Cove Fort or Bearscove Castle. It was built in 1509–10 as a single storey fortification for the purpose of protecting the harbour and also to be a second line of defence if the ones at the river mouth were taken.

Find your way through this former strongpoint and turn right and climb the flight of irregular stone steps of various rock types, which will lead you up to the road at rooftop level. Here there are such good views across to Kingswear that you may feel inclined to take a photo.

Turn right and walk down the cleverly engineered slope back towards Dartmouth's town. This is Newcomen Road, named after the inventor of the pumping engine, a road that contains more than its share of places of worship though some have obviously erred from the straight and narrow ... St Barnabas, built about 1831, was originally a chapel-of-ease of St Petrox at Dartmouth Castle. It was opened in 1831 but rebuilt in 1866. Today it's something of a second hand church or shop with an amazing collection of items. If you need spiritually uplifting it may or may not be the place to visit, depending upon your persuasions, but go and have a look for yourself.

Many of the properties in this road and overlooking the river are bed and breakfast establishments and holiday apartments. If St Barnabas isn't quite what it seemed don't be fooled by the sign for Trafalgar House because it's not a pub! Carry on downhill past the Catholic Church, which still is the catholic church of St John the Baptist, and head past the 'converted' library towards the town. It was originally a United Methodist Chapel, built in 1886. Do not bear left into Higher Street but steer a steady course towards the Harbour Bookshop, which was once owned by 'Christopher Robin'. You may recall that he was the son of A. A. Milne who took his son's toys and teddy bear and brought them to life in such classic stories as *Winnie-the-Pooh* (1926) and *The House at Pooh Corner* (1928).

Beside this bookshop is another of those little lanes, so common in Dartmouth. This is Horn Hill, one that leads up to The Cherub, a fourteenth century building. Follow it the short distance up to Higher Street and turn right to admire some of the oldest and most attractive buildings in the town. There are a few folk in Dartmouth whose memories go back to the time when there were even more in this medieval heartland of the town. Sadly despite their fine architecture, the match of anything there today, these medieval buildings had lapsed into a decayed and dangerous state. Economics ruled the day in 1925 when many buildings were demolished as part of a slum clearance scheme. The nearby St Saviour's Court survived until 1935, its dwellings being taken down before they fell down! During the Second World War a bomb that fell in Higher Street demolished a pub, called the Town Arms, and a shop. Two people were killed in this attack.

The Seven Stars may provide a temptation to tarry awhile but a visit to nearby St Saviour's Church, now seen behind the pub and dedicated in 1372, is suggested. The late

great, eminent Professor W. G. Hoskins described it as "exceptionally interesting" picking out its South Door as "remarkable" and provided the little gem of information that, "In the gallery is an early town fire engine, of which the twin is now in the Science Museum at South Kensington." This was Richard Newsham's 'engine', patented in 1725. However despite all its wondrous brasses and other features it's not the mother church of Dartmouth. St Clement, high on the hill at Townstal, holds that honour and long ago, before a chapel was permitted in the lower part of the town, the people must have thought that Heaven itself could only have been one storey higher as they struggled up the hill to worship.

On leaving the church turn right and walk around the back of it to reach Anzac

Street, which was originally Hanover Street. On the right hand side of the street is a museum of items that reflect the life and times of local man William Henley (1860–1919). A visit will give an impression of what it was like to be in Dartmouth in his time but there is much of interest as this man thrived on an enthusiasm for scientific matters. His sister opened the museum in his memory.

With the town trail now occupying a large chunk of your allotted life span carry on down to the next junction where you will see Foss Street carrying straight across. The circular clock reinforces this notion and bears the name W. H. Hole – Dartmouth. Continue along Foss Street, which is built on the line of a dam that was constructed in the thirteenth

century as a barrier to pond back water for a tidal mill. It is only in recent years that it has been pedestrianised to make it such a pleasant street to amble along. One of the joys of Dartmouth is that its town centre is not dominated by large chain store shops, the end result being some individual businesses where there are some surprising items for sale. But however appealing Foss Street is we turn left about half way along it, into the extremely short Union Street, to visit the market that was built in 1828. Although the nature of the market has changed considerably in recent decades there is still a buzz here on market days – Tuesdays and Fridays.

If it's not market day when you do this trail, and you do not wish to avail yourself of the toilet facilities, return to Foss Street and this time turn left along it to its end. So far the trail has either been mainly waterfront or town but it is the next bit the tourists don't normally see, for a number of reasons. To capture the mood and feel of Dartmouth it's well worth exploring some of the parts where people work or live. As this is Dartmouth, such a walk through a residential area is a pleasurable experience.

From the end of Foss Street cross the road to where an apparent dead end presents itself ahead of you, but appearances can be deceptive... This is Brown's Hill Steps and far from being a cul-de-sac for pedestrians it was originally the pack horse route into and out of Dartmouth. Grant's Cottage, at the bottom and on the right, which is painted in a colourful green and yellow, was renovated in 1886. In these back streets the use of window boxes and flower tubs makes for an attractive village-type scene, like a setting from "Last of the Summer Wine". A long, long staircase presents itself but with the steps several feet apart this stairway is not to Heaven, but up to the coffin-shaped 'Alma' near the top. The lane bears right to pass Alma Cottage and reach the junction of Brown's Hill and Clarence Hill. It was once quite the fashion to name buildings or bridges after the Battle of the Alma, in 1854, in the Crimean War.

You will be glad, perhaps even ecstatic, to know that this is the highest point on the walk and that anything else is either flat or downhill! Turn right and walk along the street. On the right are occasional glimpses of rooftop, town centre-Dartmouth down below. The great depression where these buildings now stand was once a tidal inlet, filled in after 1815. Remember that anything approaching flatness in this South Devon town is most likely to have been reclaimed land. Not far along, on your left, is one of the smallest wonders of Dartmouth ... The smallest house in Britain is to be found on Conwy Quay, in Gwynedd, North Wales and is a mere six feet wide at the front. Although Dartmouth cannot manage such a slim contender for the title it does have a lean dwelling with an unusual story attached to it. Number 16 Clarence Hill has been described

Dartmouth and Kingswear

as one which *"... has a façade that was built in 1629 as part of a merchant's house in another part of the town. It was moved to its present site where it looks down on the street where it once stood, after war damage had destroyed the rest of it."* It is just 8 feet wide. Nearby number 19 was formerly the Britannia Inn.

The Duke and Duchess of Clarence (later to become William IV and Queen Adelaide) visited Dartmouth in 1828, hence the name of the street.

Leaving these behind walk down the hill until a short way farther along on the right another flight of steps descends, steeply this time. The top is marked by two

metal posts, the handiwork, in 1908, of Harding, the ironmonger from Torquay. Descend Cox's Steps to pass the High House and reach the road at the bottom. Just left and opposite is the George and Dragon pub with a narrow lane, Undercliff, originally called Silver Street, running beside it. Follow this narrow thoroughfare past Silver Cottage and onto another piece of ironwork, this time suspended from aloft. The frolicking duo are 'The Dancing Beggars', probably named after some sharp rocks off the coast about two miles to the south. These feature in the book that carries on where this leaves off, *From The Dart to The Start.* Well worth buying!

Continue along the lane that ends with a right turn onto a stretch of road beside the repair shop of a garage. At Mayors Avenue turn left and proceed to the North Embankment. Here you will see many of the boats that carry passengers on river cruises. There is always a lot of activity on the water, a reason why so many like to simply sit and watch the various maritime movements. But we head south or right back towards our starting point. Opposite the public conveniences is another commemorative stone memorial titled 'For Freedom'. This records the departure from here on 3 June 1944 of an amphibious force of 485 ships of the United States Navy to take part in the invasion of Normandy. Locals didn't see too much of the intense activity as they had been ordered to stay indoors.

The liberation of the oppressed countries of North West Europe was successfully achieved but the Americans paid a high price in their training in Start Bay where a thousand men lost their lives. This memorial was unveiled on 12 July 1954 by HRH the Duke of Edinburgh.

Although we have almost finished it's still worth the effort to cross the road, veering left of the toilets, to enter the colourful Royal Avenue Gardens. From the entrance make a beeline for the bandstand. Almost immediately is another commemorative stone, this

time to Thomas Newcomen, a staunch Baptist, inventor of the atmospheric steam engine, who was born in Dartmouth in 1663. He was the first man to conceive the idea of working a piston by steam. His invention was a positive boon for both the Devon and Cornish tin mining industries as it enabled water to be pumped out of mine workings thereby allowing the extraction of tin ore to go on even in wet weather when the mines might well have been forced to cease production. A visit to the nearby Tourist Information Centre is worthwhile for housed within the same building is one such machine! All the land of this park was

Dartmouth and Kingswear

previously an island that was linked to the old quay by a bridge. It was referred to as the New Ground when it was reclaimed in 1670. The adjacent car park was a much later addition with something like 50,680 square feet being added when the Pool was infilled in 1876–77. Modern Dartmouth isn't quite what Nature had in mind!

Before your own little engine runs out of steam head on to the bandstand. It is likely that only one person in a hundred will spot the plaque that states: "This Bandstand erected by the Town Council was formally opened in association with the loyal demonstration of inhabitants of the Borough on the eve of the Coronation of King George the V by E. Lort-Phillips , 21 June 1911, Mayor ." There are not many Dartmothians still around who were there for that opening ceremony but there are still those who occasionally visit the small sundial with green beret, nearby, placed here by Number 1 Army Commando to commemorate the 50th anniversary of their formation in Dartmouth, 5 March 1941.

There are many benches in these gardens dedicated to the memories of those folk who loved sitting here in such lovely surroundings with palm trees and other subtropical plants to create an exotic atmosphere.

Nearer the entrance arch is a circular fountain with a little cherubic character gleefully spraying away. Closer scrutiny of this attractive circular feature reveals the heads of two diminutive African elephants, one on each side, complete with trunks (ideal for splashing around in water as these two do all the time!)

Stand here and look up. Above the Royal Castle Hotel is this inscription, "This old coaching inn has been famous since Drake first sailed." It could so easily say that here is an establishment haunted by a ghost that is known to have more than a passing interest in ladies underwear – to find out the intimate details of this undercover spook you will have to read *The Ghosts of Torbay*. However should you be outside the Royal Castle in the wee small hours of the morning in early November, keep an ear open for the unmistakable sound of a coach and horses riding over cobblestones here. Apparently this ghostly sound emanates from the now invisible coach sent here to carry Mary, consort of

Dartmouth and Kingswear

William III, from her accommodation to meet her husband in Torbay. Some say that the sounds have also been heard as if they come from within this wonderful old establishment.

Not many visitors notice the weather vane in the shape of a sailing vessel, on the National Westminster Bank, by local and highly gifted, blacksmith Alan Middleton. The splendid arch at the entrance (or exit) to the Royal Avenue Gardens, again by Alan Middleton, is a fine gift to the town from the Middleton family. Another plaque on it states that, "The Old Dartmothians Association are proud to be associated with this arch."

The building ahead, with all the pillars, is the Butterwalk, part of which now houses the town's museum. It was built in 1635 for a rich merchant who made his fortune from the Newfoundland trade. When it was built it was possible for ships to sail up to his back door, the land having been reclaimed since then. This is why several buildings in Dartmouth look like warehouses but are not by the water.

For those with a thirst for local knowledge or simply an interest in Dartmouth there is no finer place to visit than this museum. Don't leave it until a wet day, go and see the various collections and you'll learn a lot more about the town than this little book will ever tell you!

In the Second World War Dartmouth had its darker moments, some attacks leaving their mark on the town's history. Just one example, of many, occurred mid-morning on 13 February 1943. A German bomber wreaked havoc killing fourteen people. This episode was deeply felt in this tight knit community. The pillars propping up the

Butterwalk were damaged and it was first thought that this historic building would have to be demolished. Fortunately it has been saved to become one of the most photographed buildings in the town.

Another centre of attention is the Boatfloat, formed in 1882, where locals may recall, with affection, a delightful little character with an identity problem. 'Snowy', a little white duck, was always in the company of swans because he apparently thought of himself as an ugly swan rather than a beautiful duckling! Perhaps this story, a variation on a theme, could be the basis for a song with a happy ending. I wonder what Danny Kaye would have made of it!

With such thought-provoking ideas in your mind follow around the edge of the Boatfloat back to the starting point for a well deserved cup of tea or something, perhaps, that little bit stronger. As they might say at the Station Restaurant – just the ticket!

Having walked in and around Dartmouth town's narrow back streets and alleys let's see what other people think about Dartmouth. Here is a selection of descriptions, written at different times. You will have to make your own mind up whether or not these statements ring quite so true today.

"Dartmouth is the prettiest place in the world," so said a much-travelled film producer between the two world wars. Such a bold statement, by such a well-qualified source, was like gold dust to those entrusted with the task of promoting Dartmouth after the war. Although rationed with their use of paper they still managed to produce their official guide in 1946 starting with that quote. The statement was qualified with their own interpretation of what the film producer meant, *"It has always been known as the most beautiful estuary in the West at all seasons of the year. Neighbouring resorts are often buffeted by boisterous weather straight in from the sea, but try as it might it cannot get at Dartmouth, nestled as it is inside its landlocked harbour. And what a harbour! Few havens offer such safe anchorage for yachts; few places can cater for yachts and yachtspeople as Dartmouth can. Everything required is close at hand. The beauty of the estuary can be appreciated from a yacht as it passes in between the picturesque castles at the mouth. Each side the wooded banks run down to still waters; waters that are famous for the training of Officers of the Royal Navy and as a rendezvous for yachtspeople of distinction."*

The 1946 official guide also quoted a well known journalist of the day, Clarissa Charlesworth, who lived at Kingswear. *"I see once more – in miniature – the fairyland quality of Sydney Harbour from the windows of my new home. I have written of many beautiful spots, of buildings, of ships, of men who sail them. Here, once again, in lovely Dartmouth I am reunited with these manifold beauties ... I have now found 'Journey's End', here in your lovely country."*

That same postwar guide was also practical as well as poetic. It contained various advertisements and by simply calling the operator and obtaining the number 'Dartmouth 3' you could talk to 'The Urban Electric Supply Co. Ltd.,' who were based at 25 Fairfax Place and discuss their reasonable electricity tariffs. As their slogan so wisely and pithily pointed out, "Electricity gives satisfaction with economy."

Visitors from France, coming to an alien land with only a basic grounding in English, could rest easy after getting through on Dartmouth 128 where, at the Commercial Hotel amongst their list of wondrous claims, was the phrase "On Parle Français." Presumably Mr and Mrs Lord, the proprietors, saw the opportunity to get one step ahead of their rivals and encourage French visitors long before we came to be more greatly involved in Europe

and with 'our friends (or 'amis') across the water.'

More than three score years ago an article in the *Western Morning News* gave a description of Dartmouth, one that bears, at least in part, airing yet again. There are those who say the town has changed beyond recognition whilst others feel it has managed to stave off the worst that only progress can inflict. Judge for yourself: *"Every year thousands of tourists who are 'doing' Devon pass Dartmouth by with a hurried visit. They are satisfied with a cursory glance at a gem of peerless quality. Passing up or down the river they say 'Oh, how beautiful!' As they turn away from the wonderful vista of the peaceful old town of Dartmouth and the charming village of Kingswear both set like jewels facing each other on opposite sides of the silver river...*

Dartmouth well repays the long sojourn, for the town provides variety. The beauty of the River Dart is famed in song; the river provides boating and fishing, and there is sea bathing in the coves on either side of its mouth and within a few minutes walk from either Dartmouth or Kingswear. The Dartmouth Corporation provide lawn tennis at the courts in Victoria Road, and there are the bowling greens where visitors can enjoy a quiet afternoon with the 'woods.'

The town is restful and abounds with ancient places of interest... In these days the expense of a holiday is often considered too much for people with moderate incomes.

There are no exorbitant charges for the sundries of entertainment at Dartmouth ...
Nowadays the town is coming more and more into its rightful place as a health resort,
offering unique opportunities for a delightful holiday at a moderate cost ... Dartmouth
is sometimes called "Devon's beauty spot" – a big claim to make in a county noted
everywhere for its loveliness ... It does not need to be pointed out that, with such a variety
of subjects from which to choose, Dartmouth is a Mecca to the devotee of photographic
art. The man with a camera can make his choice between sea and river pictures, between
hill and valley scenery, and the grim old fortresses perched on their crags, not to mention
[which of course the article did!] *the chances of obtaining charming studies of half-*
timbered houses..."

The article was as long as this book is short but conveys the mood and feel of a place
that maintains a similar atmosphere. I would imagine that the major photographic
processing labs are familiar with Dartmouth, and the Dart, as visitors click away
incessantly, day in, day out to record for posterity their time, however brief, at Dartmouth.

What could be simpler in a place name than Dartmouth being at the mouth of the River
Dart? That great river of some forty miles in length rises in the mires and mists of
Dartmoor, the roof of Devon, before wending its way through some of the county's best
scenery to mingle with the tidal waters of the estuary. It gives its name to many places
along its course – Dartmeet, Dartington and the most beautiful of them all Dartmouth!

Queen Victoria did a lot of unwitting promotional work for various Devonshire rivers.
Her trip up the Tamar prompted thousands to follow in her footsteps and her visits to the
Dart also had an impact. She wrote in her journal, "It puts me much in mind of the beautiful
Rhine with its ruined castles and the Lorelei."

Of course if you accept the notion that the Dart is the 'English Rhine', albeit on a very
small scale, then a comparison can also be made between Dartmouth and the typical
settlement found along the Rhine. A writer in 1869 aired these thoughts on the matter: *"If*

the Dart be like the Rhine still more is Dartmouth a Rhenish town. The nature of its site – a brief stretch of ground backed by precipitous hills, up and along which buildings extend and the antique character of the bulk of these; render the little seaport one of the most quaintly picturesque in the West of England."

But it's the exploring of the river that is, for many, their lasting impression of the area… The *Exeter and Plymouth Gazette* of March 1836 carried a story about the introduction of the first steam ferry to ply the Dart, a pioneering venture that proved to be the forerunner of a trade that employs many local people and an enterprise that has its rival companies today, each fiercely proud of its boats and personnel. Things were a bit different as the Victorian era was about to dawn. *"The Dart is about to be navigated by a steam vessel, which we understand is now building by a subscription of one hundred shares of £20 each, the whole of which are taken, fifty shares by Dartmouth, and fifty shares by Totnes and the neighbourhood. The vessel is to be called 'The United Dart' and the company will be named 'The United Dart Steam Navigation Co.' It is intended that the vessel shall make the trip from Dartmouth to Totnes and back every morning and evening for the conveyance of goods and passengers, and in the middle of the day to be employed towing vessels in and out of the harbour."*

How different things are today! Anyone only half intending to make the journey is likely to be tempted or persuaded by the various representatives of the firms who operate the motor launches. The competition makes an entertaining spectacle at times with alternating kiosks and some slick sales talk trying to convince you that the best, no, the only, way to see 'The English Rhine' is on **their** boats.

What we would recommend is Bob Mann's excellent guide to the journey to or from Totnes. Titled *Boat Trip Down the Dart* it tells you almost everything there is to know and more than many of the river captains can relate in the time at their disposal. Should you take a shine to Totnes then you should get the indispensable *Great Little Totnes Book*. However, crossing the Dart has preoccupied many people and various cross-river ferries have come and gone.

The Mew was a funny little thing but everybody loved her and she was as brave as they came! She must have plied her way across the Dart thousands of times, hardly noticed, in her unobtrusive way but *The Mew* was a bit special for it was this diminutive little vessel that did so much sterling work in her heyday. Visitors with a long-standing sentimental attachment to the area, and long-in-the-tooth Dartmothians, remember her with great affection.

'Mew' in Devon dialect means seagull or the cry of a seagull, an apt name for this Great Western ship as she was never far from the attentions of these sea birds. Her mast head was invariably occupied by a gull as she ferried her passengers between Kingswear and Dartmouth. Captain Harris had the second best perch as he steered her from a tiny wheel house built against the single funnel. It was from this aerie that her skipper embarked on a much lengthier crossing, the one to Dunkirk. She was designed to cope with the 'lop' of estuarial inlets and not the swell of the open sea but nothing would have stopped her in her finest hour. When the hour cometh so did *The Mew*! However back in her home port of Dartmouth she performed one more heroic wartime deed and saved the blushes of the Englishman in charge of the French destroyer *The Mistral*…

Sir Martin Dunbar-Nasmith, VC, who was then Commander-in-Chief, Plymouth, cut a dashing figure as an Admiral. He decided to make an inspection of the college and when it was suggested that he be driven there he dismissed the idea out of hand. He was a naval man and he undertook to enlist *The Mistral* as his personal flagship for the short voyage up the Devon coastline. Most people in the South Hams, certainly those who live along its coastline, know what a strong south-easterly wind can do in Start Bay. By chance a devilishly strong wind blew over the briny, almost as if to remind the French vessel of what her name meant! She made it into the haven of the Dart Estuary with the noise of her sirens reverberating around the hills. However as she came abreast of the Lower Ferry she tried to go about. The manoeuvre went wrong as the winds, the tide and the unfamiliarity of the crew to the idiosyncrasies of the vessel's French engines resulted in the ship drifting hopelessly out of control. She was headed for the rocks between Warfleet and Bayards Cove and certain doom...

Meanwhile, our friend *The Mew*, who had been waiting, minding her own business, for the 9.30 from Newton Abbot, suddenly shot into action and ploughed through the choppy waters of the estuary straight for *The Mistral*. At the same time a French tug had also spotted the imminent disaster and had headed out to help as well. Somehow the unlikely

Warfleet, Dartmouth

double act managed to turn the destroyer and save the day but only after a mighty struggle that was watched by many onlookers from the safety of the shore. The acting Harbourmaster, a Welshman, was so overjoyed at this highly unlikely rescue that he did a dance for joy on the harbourside. Both the French tug and *The Mew* were acknowledged for their wonderful work, a rescue that must have saved a great admiral from acute embarrassment at having to be saved at the eleventh hour by two such relatively unglamorous craft. One of *The Mew's* forerunners was *The Dolphin*, an unusual ferry in that both the stern and the bow were pointed so that it could go in either direction.

Every good, and quite a few bad, Geography teachers will tell you that the South West Peninsular is an excellent place for studying rias. This, for the uninitiated, is a river valley that has been drowned by a rise in sea levels as a result of a warming up of the climate and a corresponding melting of the ice caps. We have many estuaries in the west country that have been submerged and form long inlets often with many branches. The consequence, even if we have fallen asleep trying to understand the concept, is a practical one as these rias have probably cost you and I a small fortune over the years! Their width and length have posed problems to communications. To bridge them is prohibitively expensive and to drive around them is a time consuming, petrol-guzzling exercise. From Kingswear to Dartmouth by main road is about 23 miles and getting through Totnes can add years to your life!

At Dartmouth the Dart is wide and deep, so we have a number of ferries or floating

bridges wearing themselves out crisscrossing the Dart to convey motorists across the river. Sitting patiently in wait for them are motorists, in all shapes and sizes their moods often reflected by how far back up the hill they are queued, be it thirty minutes, an hour or an eternity from being able to cross. Perhaps the hapless motorist can reflect on just how many person hours have been spent whiling away the time since the first ever trip was made way back in August 1831. The newspaper of the day reported the following details: *"It is impelled across the river upon chains, and being of great size and accommodation, and employed on a river of great depth and rapidity of stream, the power used to impel it on the chains is steam. It conveyed across the river, from its eastern to its western shore, a distance of 1650 feet, upwards of sixty carriages, with their horses attached, 200 horses, and five or 600 foot passengers, between the hours of one and five o'clock, on the day of opening. The bridge and roads were designed by Mr Rendell the engineer, in the latter part of the year 1829."*

We are now an island race of car owners and obviously the wait is just another of the prices we pay for the privilege. It's interesting to note this comment in a guide book to South Devon written in 1907 by C. G. Harper: "The cheapest ferry in England is that which takes you across from Kingswear to Dartmouth." How times have changed!

Those who arrive by train are not usually subjected to as long a wait and are not held to ransom with such kingly tolls or tariffs. The latter has been a bone of contention with some locals for many years and there are obviously many ways of looking at the situation. In a newspaper article from the past it stated that: "In London there was a free ferry service across the Thames and motorists had an equal right to a free passage across the Dart." There is, but it's many miles up the river at Totnes! And that too was a toll-paying bridge until the opposition got to be too much and the powers-that-be relented.

From time immemorial there has been talk of spanning the river, near Dartmouth, with a bridge. In the late 1930s three proposals were considered. One bridge could straddle the Dart near the famous Anchor Stone, where legend has it that nagging wives were often deliberately marooned in midstream till they became more meek and mild. This then would really have been 'A Bridge over Troubled Waters'! The other two structures were closer to Dartmouth – one a low span bridge near the site of the Higher Ferry, the other a high and spectacular bridge rising out of Kingswear and descending down on to Sandquay. The Dartmouth Corporation favoured the last one and put it to a higher authority but other 'minor' details like the cost of such a scheme and the advent of the Second World War knocked that one on the head!

There are many establishments that start out in a humble, even in a primitive fashion, only to develop and go on to enjoy a sophisticated and well-appointed premises. This is certainly the case in the story of the Royal Naval College

In 1863 HMS *Britannia* arrived at the port to be the training centre for naval officers. The men were subjected to conditions that were far from satisfactory and HMS *Hindustan* was brought in two years later to create more space and to add to the facilities. But life on these vessels remained cramped and unhygienic and something had to be done.

The ultimate contrast came about when Sir Aston Wood, who was the architect for the Victoria and Albert Museum, designed the college that now sits grandly on the hill above the town. But it wasn't all plain sailing, if you will excuse the maritime pun, for the owners of the land were far from happy to let such a fine site go. History was made as the land was acquired by compulsory purchase, the first acquisition of this fashion in this country! The college was built between 1899–1905. Its foundation stone was laid by King Edward VII in 1902. Today it stands dominating the scene high above the town and the trade it

generates locally is an important factor in the fortunes of Dartmouth.

Although the building had its critics its heritage is almost unparalleled in so short a time span with so many great men having passed through there. Royalty has graced its portals on many occasions and it can be argued that the Royal Naval College has played its part in shaping the history of this country, in no small way. It was here, in July 1939, that the Queen first set eyes on Prince Philip. George VI came in on the royal yacht *Victoria and Albert* and with him was the young Princess Elizabeth. She was about fourteen and Philip, some five years older, was training at the college.

Many royals have been trained at Dartmouth and these go back to 1872 when the sons of the Prince of Wales, George and Albert, endured the dubious delights of HMS *Britannia* and HMS *Hindustan*. In their footsteps, to Dartmouth, followed Edward VIII, George VI, Prince Philip, Prince Charles and Prince Andrew.

HMS *Hindustan* (along with HMS *Impregnable*) has survived in an unusual way and is hardly recognisable as the incredible hulk that she was in her Dartmouth days. Her timbers were salvaged and used in the famous Liberty's building in Regent Street/ Marlborough Street in London. The designs of Edwin T. Hall and E. Stanley Hall were influenced by the distinctive Rows of Chester and they contrived to use the salvaged teak on the exterior and the oak on the inside making good use out of the remains of these two grand old 'men-of-war'. The timbers were properly mortised and tenoned on the outside but reinforced by a brick backing.

The setting of Dartmouth with its steep hills as a backcloth has left an impression on many observers, not least an Italian spy long ago doing some reconnaissance work for a possible second attempted invasion fleet or Armada. When quizzed about Dartmouth's defences he explained that: "Dartmouth is not walled; the mountains are its walls." Anyone who has had to walk up these slopes will know exactly what the spy meant!

However, Dartmouth also has some extremely strong man-made defences. Dartmouth Castle, open to the public, is at the mouth of the river and well worth visiting.

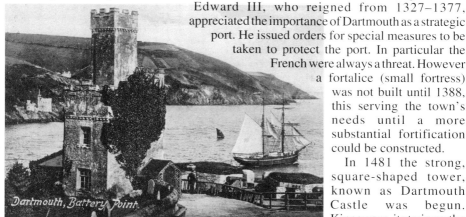

Edward III, who reigned from 1327–1377, appreciated the importance of Dartmouth as a strategic port. He issued orders for special measures to be taken to protect the port. In particular the French were always a threat. However a fortalice (small fortress) was not built until 1388, this serving the town's needs until a more substantial fortification could be constructed.

In 1481 the strong, square-shaped tower, known as Dartmouth Castle was begun. Kingswear, its twin on the opposite bank, was commenced a decade later and cost a staggering £68 to build (no mention of VAT then!). The materials for these stout stone edifices were brought by barges from the slate quarries at Charleton near Kingsbridge. The Tower of the old Chantry at Slapton was from the same source. A large quantity of stone was also brought from Cornworthy, a small hilltop village above Bow Creek.

As soon as possible another outlay of £14 was lavished on the castle. This time two great 'murderers' were employed, not of the human-type but guns to achieve the same fatal outcome on its targets.

From the year 1504 the name of Holdsworth was synonymous with the maintenance of Dartmouth Castle. Several successive members of the family held the title of Governor and a stipend of forty pounds was paid each year to see that it was kept in a good state of

repair. Another requirement was that the chain – sometimes referred to as 'Old Jawbones' – which stretched between Dartmouth Castle and the fort at Godmerock, a short distance north of Kingswear Castle, kept out enemy ships by night or, on specific occasions, was sufficiently taut in order to truly trip them up! The condition was couched in these wonderful words "a cheyne sufficient in length and strength to streche and be laide overthwarte or a travers the mouthe of the haven of Dartmouth." It is believed that the chain was linked to Godmerock because it was the best point of anchorage.

However as the years passed by the chain fell into disuse and as this reduced the workload the stipend was similarly reduced. However given the cost of living in those days and the limited requirements of the job it still would have been a 'nice little earner'.

In the Second World War, as part of the coastal defences, a new, improved, and more sophisticated version of the chain was installed across the Dart to keep out U-boats. This was steel cables, manoeuvred into place by a sturdy little vessel.

The visitor can learn much about Dartmouth's ancient history by a tour of the castle and St Petrox Church. The latter has an east window to the memory of George Parker Bidder who was famous for being 'The Calculating Boy'. You can read more about him in *From The Dart to The Start.*

The outlook from Dartmouth Castle, on a fine summer's day, is a particularly pleasing one to behold. It is a colourful scene, an ever changing view with a veritable fleet of small craft in and out of the Dart passing safely with no chain to halt them in their course.

Devon, lying along the English Channel, has always been more wary of invading forces than landlocked counties well away from these shores. A story occurs in several locations in Devon that in the absence of troops on hand to defend us against the French, in Napoleonic times, if a vessel was spotted in the channel that might be carrying potential invading forces the ladies of the district would spring into action. Donning red coats or cloaks they would grab stout sticks or brooms (like some fearsome Napoleonic Nora Batty!) and position themselves on some prominent landmark to give the impression of a regiment. This, then, had the effect of making any would-be attackers think twice before coming ashore. Such a ploy was used at Sidbury in East Devon (see *Around and About Sidmouth*) and is believed to have been done at Gallants Bower, a great buttress above the mouth of the Dart.

Throughout the years bonfires have lit the skies of Devon. In Armada times a chained network was set up across the country so that a warning of a possible invasion could be passed around the realm in a matter of hours instead of the weeks it would have taken messengers to reach every hamlet, village or town. All along the coast or close to it are hills called Beacon Hill and the act of lighting fires has been rekindled for other more peaceful events like coronations and jubilees. A bonfire on the Gallant Estate, near the mouth of the Dart was constructed in 1935, a Bonfire Committee supervising a troop of boy scouts in their potentially dangerous task. This great pyre had a diameter of twenty feet, a circumference of sixty feet and rose some thirty feet above the ground. To make sure it was a bonfire that was going to be seen five tons of coal, twenty tons of timber, 200 gallons of tar and forty gallons of oil were included. (Hope someone remembered to bring the matches!) This beacon was alight for twenty four hours and its effect could be seen illuminating the night sky from as far afield as Totnes, Torquay, and Brixham. As part of the same celebrations there were smaller bonfires lit at the Royal Naval College, Stoke Fleming, Kingswear, Blackawton, and Dittisham (pronounced Ditsum!)

In those days there was little flat land between the base of these steep hills and the river so this would have emphasised the feature. Almost all the flat land in Dartmouth, as we have seen, has been reclaimed with numerous examples of man's ingenuity in creating new space out of a marshy or muddy terrain. The Coombe Mud, a delicate shade of embellished brown, was enclosed in the 1930s as the new North Embankment afforded easier access from the Higher Ferry to the town. Today that enclosed area is Coronation Park. Hidden beneath the grassy, sporting venue are the hulks of rusting ships and even a German submarine, so if you see a periscope popping up amongst any soccer players you will know from whence it came! Certainly it would give a more literal meaning to the soccer term "bringing on the sub!"

In the Second World War this open space was covered by Nissen huts. These accommodated American troops who were stationed at Dartmouth whilst preparing for the Normandy landings.

In a town that has seen more royalty than is found in a pack of cards, no less than seven reigning monarchs have wined and dined at the Royal Castle Hotel. And it was never a problem when choosing a name for the local 'flea pit'. Dartmouth's three hundred-seater 'Royalty Cinema' was functional rather than ornate, the architect not being swayed by the art deco style of cinema so common throughout the region. Today it is just a memory as the demolition men made swift work of it in the early 1980s. Some people walking by claim to hear the ghostly sounds of stomping feet and clapping hands, the inevitable response that followed every occasion when the film broke. To run a cinema of the type of the Royalty you either needed to be an eternal optimist or have it dictated by your genetic make-up for there was never financially much reward in it. Kelvin White gave it a go between 1963–73 and had, with his brother Grenville, run the doomed Romany Cinema at Totnes. This closed its doors to the public in 1964, no doubt in response to a dearth of good films and a vast increase in television viewing figures.

Charles Scott, who had a wealth of experience in similar places of entertainment, took the helm but a drastic proposed rent rise put paid to the Royalty and the South Hams lost a cinema that had served it well for a great many years. There were the inevitable protests

and a two thousand signature petition included some notable signatures like that of international film star Donald Sutherland, but all to no avail. On the previous page it is shown after its closure but prior to its demolition.

Dartmouth and the area in its immediate vicinity has been used for location shooting for a number of television programmes, feature films and television commercials. My book *Made in Devon* covers this for the whole of the county so if this section about Dartmouth and Kingswear whets your appetite then I suggest you get a copy. Many famous household names have been to this South Devon town but if they have been totally absorbed in their roles they would have convinced themselves that they were elsewhere for Dartmouth and the river has been the Amazon and its jungle, Scotland, Liverpool, Germany and a host of other places and has been taken back in time, probably more times than even Dr Who! There has even been the odd X-rated film…

The Sailor Who Fell From Grace With The Sea, a title that blatantly bucks the trend of slick one, two, or three word titles to catch the attention of the would-be cinema-goer, contained scenes that shocked some Dartmothians when they eventually saw it. However one or two old codgers were too busy looking at the scenery to notice! Film critic, Benny Green noticed and in *Punch* amusingly wrote, "This everyday tale of torture, scopophilia, copulation, masturbation, dismemberment and antique dealing deserves to be traded back to the Japs [it was based on a novel by Yukio Mishima] and made required viewing for timorous kamikaze pilots." Since that was written some years ago the Japanese have discovered the delights of *Endurance,* a one word title for something just as excruciating if not quite in the same league as this film made in Dartmouth and starring Kris Kristofferson and Sarah Miles. The film relates the drastic measures undertaken by the son of a widow who hopes to develop a romance with a sailor by castrating him. Kris Kristofferson endeared himself by mingling in the local community when off the set and entertained a local audience at a folk club with his passable impersonation of that ever-cheerful (!) contemporary folk singer Leonard Cohen.

You would have to have a long memory to recall a film called *The Lonely Road* that was

made in the 1930s in and around Dartmouth. Its stars were Clive Brook and Victoria Hopper, who were famous in their day, and the entire crew stayed at the Raleigh Hotel (shown opposite). A wedding scene was shot at Dartmouth Castle, the beautiful bride being a local girl called Jean Trowson. The film was set in the hey-days of smuggling and Blackpool Sands, specially illuminated for the occasion, was used for the night scenes. No doubt in the past it was the scene of real-life nefarious activities such as this! More detail can also be found in *From The Dart to The Start*.

Agatha Christie was born Agatha Mary Clarissa Miller at Torquay on 15 September 1890. She was a lady whose stories have baffled, bemused, beguiled and bewitched millions of people over a great many years and her stories have frequently featured places in this part of Devon. She lived for many years on the banks of the River Dart, at Greenway, opposite Dittisham and she loved the scenery.

Many of her stories involved murder and she created enough victims to fill an entire graveyard, I suspect. One of them was found, but only in a literary sense, in her boathouse in the story *Dead Man's Folly*, written in 1956. However she unwittingly passed up an opportunity to give local tourism a boost when she chose the Nile rather than the Dart for one of her most famously dramatised thrillers. 'Death on the Dart' would even have had that extra little bit of alliteration, presenting a title that would have put this much smaller river on the world map.

Although she passed away in 1976, many of her stories have continued to be used for both television and films, some having not only been set in Devon but also filmed here…

Ordeal By Innocence is an Agatha Christie story, published in 1958 and made into a feature film, more than quarter of a century later, in 1984. It was filmed in Dartmouth where the book was set, a stone's throw from the great thriller writer's home at Greenway. Agatha heavily disguised the true identity of the place by calling it Drymouth and as it turned out such a choice of name was prophetic for the filming coincided with a rare drought and a lot of water hoses and watering cans were needed for some scenes! It had an all star cast that included Donald Sutherland in the lead with support from Ian McShane, Michael Elphick, Faye Dunaway, Sarah Miles (yet again!), Annette Crosbie and Christopher Plummer, who had also been to Devon to film *International Velvet*, some six years earlier, in 1978. In one sequence Donald Sutherland is seen inside the Torbay Cinema in Paignton but as he runs out, hey presto, it is magically the Royalty at

Dartmouth. Lots of locations were used in and around the town but the film was greeted less enthusiastically than was hoped: "Cast wasted, logic absent in utterly pointless film" stated Leonard Malting's movies guide.

Bearing in mind Dartmouth's long affinity with the Navy it is entirely appropriate that a film about Lord Nelson should include several scenes shot at Dartmouth. *Bequest To The Nation* concentrated more on Nelson's extra-curricular activities rather than his daring deeds in sea battles. The film was based on a Terence Rattigan play. The beginning and end sequences were filmed at Dartmouth whilst, in between, Nelson was embroiled in his passionate relationship with Lady Hamilton. This interpretation gave the impression that the Lady in question was no lady. The Americans retitled the film *The Nelson Affair*. One of the few sea battles in the film was shot indoors! Involved in this cinematic portrayal were Glenda Jackson, Anthony Quayle, Nigel Stock and Peter Finch and a host of local extras employed for their seamanship skills.

Meanwhile in Kingswear more deceit was afoot in the shape of the local railway station purporting to be 'Exeter' in 1867 for the film *The French Lieutenant's Woman*. The necessity for this con lay in the unsuitability of Exeter to be as it was in the Victorian times when John Fowles set his novel.

Again the film had some big names with Leo Mckern (alias Rumpole of The Bailey) Jeremy Irons and Meryl Streep. But the elements are no respecters of stardom and despite the glittering cast the weather was far from glittering! So with the Heavens opening up and the rain cascading down a sequence was filmed at the station. But before it could all be wrapped up and safely in the can, the day drew to a close, as regards filming. Naturally everyone anticipated another wet day to complete the shoot, but the weather gods seized upon the opportunity to show what absolute swine they can be by creating a fine sunny one!

Not to be outdone, the film crew scratched their heads and came up with a contingency plan. Thus it was that a local fire crew was taken on to spray, with hoses, the station roof and environs for the duration of the shoot. To get all the right 'shots' the train arriving at 'Exeter' had to arrive no less than fourteen times!

Outside the station extensive alterations were made for the sake of authenticity. Rubber cobblestones lined the street up to the Steam Packet, most of the buildings were repainted and the Royal Dart was painted in the brown and cream of the Great Western Railway.

Another film crew to visit the area around Dartmouth were given the task of turning E. M. Forster's novel *Howard's End* into a visually stunning presentation. Sir Anthony Hopkins came to Dartmouth shortly after starring in the immensely successful *Silence of the Lambs*. The film also starred another Oscar-winning performer, Emma Thompson who was full of praise for the gorgeous scenery, as so she should!

But it's not just the big screen that has seen the potential of Dartmouth and Kingswear for many television programmes and television commercials have used this lovely scenery as a backcloth. The best known, nationally and internationally must be *The Onedin Line*, of which there were two series several years apart. It is widely believed that the locations aged less than the actors. However if you watch the episodes there are all sorts of contradictions as Dartmouth and Exeter shared the role of nineteenth century Liverpool. In one shot you see characters stood on Exeter Quay waving to a departing vessel bound for some foreign shore only to see the vessel they are waving to, two seconds later, sailing out of the Dart – forty miles away!

If you are looking for an amusing anecdote to sum up the plight of those who are charged with portraying exotic locations but do not have the budget to get as far as them then this is it! In the second series tropical rain forests were called for in the script. However as intense heat and oppressive humidity cannot be felt on film the makers thought they would get away with the dense woods along the eastern side of the Dart Estuary as a suitable jungle. To convince the audience, strategically placed crocodiles, operated by extras, gave that touch of tropical reality. Indeed all went well and everyone was delighted with the overall effect. Unfortunately if you look closely, at one episode, you will just about be able to detect, in the deep, dense jungle clouds of billowing steam, not from forest fires of tribal Indians, but from the Paignton and Dartmouth Steam Railway's chuffing train on its way down to Kingswear!

Well-known television chef, Keith Floyd, owns a pub on one of the inlets of the Dart Estuary. He too introduced some life-sized, even lifelike but equally lifeless, crocodiles to these waters but met with a barrage of protest, various reasons being offered as to why these shouldn't be allowed to remain there.

John Thaw has enjoyed a long and fruitful career in television in a number of key roles starring in series such as *The Sweeney, Inspector Morse* and *A Year in Provence*. He didn't spend quite that long in the Dartmouth area but stayed long enough, in 1979, to play his part as Sir Francis Drake in *Drake's Venture*. Locations all along the South Devon coast were used and the camera crew dreaded the scenes shot on the high seas for they all, to a man, suffered chronic seasickness. They were particularly concerned about this as one of their colleagues had died from this whilst filming the return of Sir Francis Chichester. The coast at Stoke Fleming played the part of the southern tip of South America.

Some four years later another seafaring saga was shot in Dartmouth and in Kingswear – *The Master of Ballantrae*. The original film version, made in 1953, starred Errol Flynn, an actor noted for playing big parts! The story was an old one, penned by Robert Louis Stevenson in 1889, some five years before he died from tuberculosis at the age of just 44. This production had its own big guns in the shape of Michael York, Timothy Dalton, Brian Blessed and Sir John Gielgud.

This Scottish saga featured the fortunes of two brothers deciding to join Bonnie Prince Charlie's 1745 rebellion. This time, Bayards Cove, at

Dartmouth was a Scottish fishing village. The ensemble stayed at the Royal Dart Hotel at Kingswear and it appears that there were a number of hilarious cock-ups at crucial moments in the filming. *Made in Devon* features some of them. Ballantrae is on the south-west coast of Scotland, north of Stranraer, but south of the small seaside resort of Girvan. Although the surrounding scenery is beautiful, this small village with a busy coast road running through its heart, is no place itself to make films, whereas Dartmouth with its preserved buildings will continue to be used as a location for period pieces.

Dartmouth showed its adaptability with a variation on a theme for *The Bell Run* when it again played a Scottish settlement but this time moved from the west coast to the east to miraculously become Aberdeen. Both sides of the Dart shared the honours with the Kingswear side seeing the bulk of the filming. Of course there have been many more productions made here and many more stories but that is another book and you know which one!

It's doubtful, though, whether any of the plots for these film and television productions are as imaginative or bizarre as a ghost story surrounding Mount Boone. Squire Boon was an unhappy man, in 1677, for two reasons. Firstly he was dismayed by his daughter's choice for a prospective husband and, secondly, he had just died! Squire Boone had, at least, extracted a promise, having used extreme threats, from his daughter that she wouldn't wed this man and could rest easily in his grave… Until, some six months later, she could no longer accept the situation so married the man. Now where would you set up the matrimonial home given the extent of harassment that she received when her father was alive? Not in the ancestral home methinks! But that's what she did and it wasn't long before the ghost of Squire Boone was on the prowl. He manifested himself by appearing with a trail of burning flames glowing in his wake. Sometimes he summoned up enough power to raise heavy pieces of furniture well off the ground and these too joined in his unhappy procession around the house. The newly weds were at their wits end so ran away to London, only to be followed by the grim spectre of Squire Boone. Things though got even worse when they returned to Dartmouth. Someone suggested an exorcism, at which Squire Boone made a guest, or should we say 'ghost', appearance. He agreed to go quietly if his daughter would go with him!

The story then moves to the nearby millstream where more wheeling-dealing took place. More conditions were introduced that gave the Squire the task of emptying this inlet with a cockleshell to achieve his goal. Presumably he found some way of achieving the impossible for three months later his daughter died!

Kingswear is more than just a location that lives on a reputation as being somewhere else. It has many associations with the sea from famous sailors through to smuggling. There have been numerous examples of hidey holes being 'discovered' in old properties. Possibly the most spectacular was in the late 1920s when a boy with a butterfly net thrust it into a hole in the ground at Kittery Court, a house with a monastic past. There was no resistance as the stick slid deep into the hole and the lad went running to tell his father. Excavations revealed a room of some fourteen feet, or so, in depth and some twelve feet in width. The fact that it was concealed beneath several feet of earth, complete with trees and long established shrubs seems to suggest a connection with smuggling as a stone trap door was found in the ceiling. The house has another claim to fame as its name was taken, in 1635, to America and was given to a town in Maine – which remains a main town in Maine!

The countryside around Dartmouth is beautiful, the trip up to Totnes or around to Brixham being the best way to see it. Driving around can be frustrating as the roads are twisty and have the typical high hedgerows so prevalent in the South Hams. Cycling the lanes is another option but the landscape of flat topped hills is carved up by deep, steep valleys. Unless you are very fit you will end up walking up most of the hills and hanging on for dear life when riding down them! That leaves walking. Fortunately there are many public rights of way in the vicinity of Dartmouth and Kingswear. The most spectacular and enjoyable romps are along the coast on both sides of the mouth of the Dart. The same applies to the steepness of many sections and you will need reserves of stamina to get the best out of a walk. Those with cars could park at or near Dartmouth Castle and head southwards towards France. The coast path passes such emotive names as Deadman's Cove (there is also a Deadman's Cross, on the outskirts of Dartmouth, names even Dame Agatha would have liked!) and Compass Cove, where to get around it you have to walk

south-west, north-west, and then south. In reality it's a lot less complicated than this sounds and the scenery is magnificent. The path is relatively easy to follow all the way to Coombe Point where it's possible to look back towards the mouth of the Dart and appreciate just how beautiful this section of cliff walking is whilst making sure not to tumble off the precipice above Shiglehill Cove. A little farther along the grassy path is Warren Point complete with a commemorative stone that tells us the good ladies of the Women's Institute purchased this bit of coast for the National Trust.

The view is now along the arc of beautiful Start Bay with Stoke Fleming in the foreground and Start Point finishing things up! From here the coast path leaves the cliffs opting to cross fields. At the large National Trust car parks turn right to Little Dartmouth. The way back to Dartmouth is along a pleasant, elevated and well signposted bridle path with even better coastal views. For less than the price of five miles you get a great little walk.

The east bank of the river mouth has some equally splendid scenery and some even steeper and longer rises and falls. These are caused by a number of small streams that have cut deep valleys down to the water's edge. They add to the enjoyment of a stroll from Kingswear in the direction of Berry Head but have the habit of making what looks like a stroll of an hour or so over an apparently short distance into a much longer drawn out affair. You can read a humorous account of a classic example of a walk along these cliffs in *Diary of a Devonshire Walker*. Just remember to carry enough energy giving foods; chocolate, glucose or mint cake are all excellent for when you have eaten them you will have less to carry and therefore be able to walk more quickly! The 1:25000 map is the best way to plan and tailor your own walks but examine the contour lines first and allow plenty of extra time or lunch will become dinner, dinner will become supper, and supper will probably mean the search and rescue groups!

From Kingswear a stroll to the Day Mark is recommended. This hollow, stone, daytime-only navigational aid and Grade II listed building, stands on the highest ground in the district. It was built in 1864 by the Dart Harbour Commissioners who retain ownership. Nevertheless access up to it is permitted via a footpath.

From that high point is a remarkable view along Start Bay with its own colourful history. It includes a number of small communities struggling along life's path but with the consolation of living in the loveliest part, of England's most beautiful county.

Away in the distance is Dartmoor, where the river that gives the name to our town is born in a kingdom of mists and mires. From the roof of Devon on those upland moors, it wends its way in a general southerly direction, all the time adding to its flow with a multitude of smaller tributaries. By the time its waters have mingled with the arm of the tide at Totnes it's become a river with which to be reckoned. Below the 'Good Town of Totnes' it opens up into a broad estuary with the steep, often wooded, slopes that gave rise to its nickname 'The English Rhine'.

And if you have been on one of those Dart cruises you will be more than familiar with the loveliness of the green countryside as the river twists and turns before finally setting eyes on Dartmouth and Kingswear, almost at the end of the river's journey and certainly at the end of this little book's.

We hope that you have enjoyed reading about some of the more unusual aspects of these places and that you have been convinced, like the film maker we mentioned earlier, that this really is "The prettiest place in the world!"

Dartmouth and Kingswear